Say No To Body Shaming

By

Elizabeth Stones

Table of content

Introduction

Growing up I have experienced what it feels like to be body shamed, coming to school everyday and having your fellow students laughing and making fun of you.
I remember asking my mom if I have always been this small, at age sixteen I looked like I was ten. I couldn't do anything with my age mates, whenever there was a party I was never invited. They called me a little girl because I was small and thin. I hated my body so much, I started doing so many things so I will be taller and maybe add more meat to my bones. At age eighteen nothing changed, I couldn't go out on a date like every young girl will do. I got mocked, and laughed at. Some called me a child including those students I knew I was older than. At home my two Junior brothers talked down on me, making me feel less of myself.

Whenever I go out with them people do ask if I was the Junior as well as the senior. It continued until I was ready for college, I was twenty but still small and thin. I couldn't make many friends in high school but in college I couldn't make any friends in my first two months.

Until I met Lilly, Lilly was a nineteen year old girl, tall, huge and fat but she didn't care what people had to say about her. When I saw her, I saw the opposite of me but she didn't care. She was always smiling and living her life. I was afraid of talking to her but I did anyway, and she was nothing but sweet. We became close friends, Lilly told me she used to be like me hating her body and wishing she was slim and not chubby. She said she never like going to parties or anywhere public until the day she saw a girl with the ideal body she wanted being mocked and body shamed, she said she then knew that people will always talk.

If you are too beautiful or ugly people will talk, if you are too small,or tall people will talk. Then she said to me, why live your life to impress when you can learn how to love your body the way it is. Her words changed my life and I started practising self love. Lilly told me to stand in front of the mirror and say that I am beautiful and nobody is more beautiful than I am. She said say it every morning until you believe it.

I was once a victim of body shaming and I overcame it. I will not say it is easy but I am happy I tried, I am happy I never gave up on myself and today, I don't care about my body size. I live my life and I am happy with myself.

You may experience feelings of anxiety, embarrassment, and self-consciousness as a result of hearing negative comments about your appearance. This can have an impact on your body image. However, there are strategies that can be utilised to effectively manage negative comments and promote overall body acceptance.

Chapter 1

The meaning of body shaming

Embarrassing someone by making improper or derogatory comments about their physical size or shape is an example of the practice known as "body shaming." You could be subjected to "body shaming," which refers to the practice of making derogatory comments about a person's weight, as well as insults that are directed toward a particular body area.

against themselves or toward other people. It's possible that you harshly assess yourself because you're unhappy with your weight or the way your body looks. You can even find yourself saying things to yourself that are negative, such as "I feel so fat today" or "I need to quit stuffing my face with food."

It is possible for your parents, siblings, friends, or even people you are not particularly close to engage in the practice of body shaming. This behavior can take place in person or remotely through the use of the internet and social media.

Body shaming occurs whenever someone criticizes another person's eating habits or the quantity of food they consume, even if they do it in jest. To shame someone's body in any way, whether intentionally or unintentionally, is to criticise their eating habits or praise their weight loss. Even though they don't intend to, your friends and family members may make statements that are critical of you, even though they don't mean to hurt your feelings. It's possible that they are unaware of the potentially damaging impact that questions such as "Have you lost weight? " or "Is it absolutely necessary for you to consume all of that? " is able to have.

the quantity of food they consume, even if they do it in jest. To shame someone's body in any way, whether intentionally or unintentionally, is to criticize their eating habits or praise their weight loss. Even though they don't intend to, your friends and family members may make statements that are critical of you, even though they don't mean to hurt your feelings. It's possible that they are unaware of the potentially damaging impact that questions such as "Have you lost weight? " or "Is it absolutely necessary for you to consume all of that? " is able to have.

Even while everyone is subject to the demands of society to present themselves in a specific manner, it is never appropriate for anyone to make comments on your physical appearance. There are strategies to overcome the problem of body shaming, establish body positivity, and learn to look at yourself in a way that is more compassionate and realistic, regardless of whether the shame is coming from yourself or from others.

Body shaming can have a range of different effects on different people. According to research, body shaming can lead to mental health issues such as depression, body dissatisfaction, low self-esteem, anxiety, and an increased risk of suicidal thoughts, as well as unhealthy behaviors such as eating disorders and excessive exercising.

Different Methods of Body Shaming

The phrase "You shouldn't wear that dress until you lose weight" is an example of fat shaming.
The phrase "She definitely needs to eat a cheeseburger" is an example of body shaming.
Criticizing someone's attractiveness by saying, "What is a girl like her doing with a guy who looks like that?" is an example of attractiveness shaming.
Disparaging comments about people's body hair, such as "Gross, underarm hair on women is such a turnoff."
Criticizing someone's eating habits by saying things like "Are you sure you want dessert? You could stand to go without."
The phrase "He's a male, he needs to bulk up more" is an example of gender shaming.

Chapter 2

The root causes of body shame

Our "selfie" culture places an emphasis on outer appearance, and we are continuously inundated with images of glamorous celebrities in various forms of media such as publications, advertising, television shows, and other types of content.

inundated with images of glamorous celebrities in various forms of media such as publications, advertising, television shows, and other types of content.

What you see on TikTok, Facebook, and Instagram on a daily basis can obviously lead you to feel envy of other people or cause you to concentrate your thoughts on your physical appearance and any perceived shortcomings you may have. You may find that it is difficult to live up to these expectations, and as a result, you may evaluate yourself harshly and have bad sensations. This can become detrimental when it lowers your sense of self-worth and the picture you have of your body.

A preoccupation with one's appearance might lead to the formation of unrealistic expectations that are impossible to fulfill. Even if you are aware that these idealized images have been digitally altered or enhanced, it is still very easy to fall into the trap of negatively comparing yourself or others to these images and conclude that you do not measure up.

Body shaming among young people

Shaming based on appearance, weight, or appearance alone is harmful to anyone, but it can be especially damaging to adolescents. The attitudes and beliefs that you develop during your teenage years with regard to your body image and your level of self-esteem are heavily influenced by your family members, peers, and social media. For their daughters, for example, mothers frequently serve as models worthy of emulation. If your mother is constantly complaining about her own shape or weight, or pointing out problems in how you look or eat, it is bound to have an impact on how you view yourself. For example, if your mother is constantly pointing out problems in how you look or eat, it is bound to have an impact.

It's perfectly normal to become extremely sensitive to remarks about your body shape, weight, and appearance as you go through the development process of adolescence. Bullying adolescents because of their weight can contribute to negative body perceptions and preoccupations with particular parts of the body when they are adolescents. Those adolescents who are particularly vulnerable are those who are overweight, and this vulnerability can frequently result in depression.

You might believe that body shaming primarily affects teenage girls, but it can also happen to boys. They can be especially worried about not being masculine enough in terms of the prevalent definition of masculinity.

Chapter 3

Effect of body shaming

Even prima ballerinas and supermodels have insecurities and flaws, but we still have a tendency to view them as the pinnacle of beauty. If you don't live up to these expectations, you could feel unworthy and insufficient. Additionally, being subjected to body shaming by others and taking their criticisms to heart can result in undesirable actions and mental health issues like:

Mood Disorders

One of the biggest risk factors for developing disordered eating or an eating disorder, such as anorexia, bulimia, or binge eating, is having a low body image.

To alter your body's shape or size, you might adopt a diet that calls for restrictive eating. However, such dieting can lead to unhealthy habits including skipping meals, fasting, post-meal vomiting, excessive exercise, or excessive laxative use.Over time, you wind up denying your body and brain of key nutrients that are important for overall health.

Disparaging remarks about a person's appearance, such as "Have you lost weight? It's possible that hearing "You look so much better" could be a trigger that leads to further disordered eating habits in an effort to either keep the weight off or lose even more weight.

Disorder of the Body Dysmorphic (BDD)

The experience of being shamed about one's body can have a negative impact on one's self-image and cause one to feel highly self-conscious. This can progress into body dysmorphic disorder, a condition in which a person becomes obsessed with a perceived imperfection in their appearance, which can lead to recurrent behaviors of avoiding that flaw.

Your day-to-day life could become overwhelmed by worries about a problem that is either minor or not readily evident to other people. You might spend a lot of time looking at yourself in the mirror or try to avoid them altogether. You might also try to hide parts of your body that you don't like, pick at your skin, or ask other people a lot of questions about how you look.

If you are continually ashamed of your physique, it might not only affect your performance in school but also your relationships with your classmates, teachers, and members of your family. Your anxiety about being evaluated by other people could lead you to avoid or cut back on your participation in social activities.

Body dysmorphic disorder (often referred to as BDD)

If you have severe symptoms of BDD, you may find that you are unable to manage the consistent level of discomfort and must thus withdraw from school as a result. You end up having suicidal thoughts and being depressed.

Excessive Exercising

In most cases, one of the finest things you can do for your health and overall well-being is to engage in activities that require physical movement. However, if it becomes an addiction and you engage in compulsive exercising, this can lead to persistent fatigue, injuries, and susceptibility to illness. Additionally, it can trigger anxiousness, depression, or irritability in the individual.

If you have a problem with obsessive exercising, you can find that your primary attention is on the activity to the point where it causes you to withdraw from other people and their company. Intense physical activity can lead to a condition known as relative energy deficiency in sport (RED-S), which manifests itself when a person's calorie consumption is insufficient in comparison to the amount of energy that they are spending in order to keep their healthy functioning intact.

Anxiety disorders and depressive states

Shaming people about their bodies can either bring on anxiety and sadness or make their symptoms worse if they already have them. If you have been subjected to public or online body shaming, such as on social media, you might want to avoid attending to school or other circumstances where you might be subjected to similar treatment. You could isolate yourself from other people, causing you to feel lonely and isolated.

Hearing disparaging comments about one's appearance can be embarrassing, bring about an increase in one's feelings of insecurity, and be damaging to one's sense of self-esteem. As a consequence of this, you might engage in critical dialogue with yourself as you internalize these sentiments of insignificance. It's possible that you've been telling yourself things like, "I'm a terrible person" or "I'm absolutely worthless." This can eventually lead to feelings of intense isolation, despair, anxiety, and a bad impression of one's body.

Concerns Relating to the Body

The stigma of fat shaming, in particular, is pervasive in our culture because of the negative connotations that are attached to obesity, such as being lazy, unattractive, and lacking the motivation to lose weight. According to the findings of one study, more than seventy percent of adolescents claimed that they had been bullied in the preceding few years because of their weight. Both your physical and mental health could suffer as a result of this action.

Shaming people for their weight has the reverse of the desired impact, which is to discourage weight loss and make people feel worse about themselves. A decrease in physical activity and an increase in calorie consumption have both been connected to the stress that the individual was experiencing.

Being the object of prejudice and discrimination based on one's weight can also have an effect on one's metabolism, lead to more weight gain, and raise the likelihood of one becoming obese. This, in turn, can increase the risk factors for a variety of physical health problems, including high blood pressure, high cholesterol, heart disease, type 2 diabetes, and others.

Chapter 4

How to change negative body talk into a positive body image

In recent years, there has been a concerted effort to reverse the emphasis on body shaming and promote more love and acceptance of how we look. Specifically, this has taken the form of efforts to: Hashtags promoting body positivity have been used on social media platforms in an effort to increase the number of followers they have and to help overcome the appearance-based prejudices that have been engrained in us.

Changing long-held ideas about what constitutes beauty will, of course, take some time. These signals have been taken in by each of us in a manner that is specific to our own cultural values, beliefs, and customs. According to the proverb, "beauty is in the eye of the beholder," and the same is true for how we perceive different forms and proportions of the human body. [Citation needed]

The pursuit of self-acceptance and the acceptance of others is an ongoing part of practising body positivity. Learning to have compassion for oneself and changing deeply ingrained cultural views takes time, patience, and practice. You have no power over what other people think or say, but you can work on shifting your thinking away from an all-or-nothing framework and beginning to see yourself as a complete individual.

If you want to overcome body shaming and create body acceptance, you can find help by following these basic steps:

- Cultivate self-love.
- Replace negative self-talk.
- Take control of the amount of time you spend on social media.
- Acquaint yourself with the food.
- Reach out to a reliable friend or family member for advice and assistance.

Cultivate self-love

Stop giving yourself a hard time about your appearance and work on developing some self-compassion as the first steps toward protecting yourself from being subjected to body shaming. It is important to keep in mind that the state of your health is more important than how you look physically, and this should be your primary focus at all times.

Don't keep to yourself or cut yourself off from other people. Do not let the fact that you are not feeling or looking your best today undermine your self-esteem or your sense of worth; this is something that happens to all of us. Take a step back and give some thought to the essential conversation that you are having with yourself inside. Is this a realistic portrayal of who you are in the real world? When you gaze in the mirror and feel hate for your face or your physique, tell yourself "no," even if you feel like you have no choice.

You should show yourself the same amount of compassion and understanding that you would for a close friend. Taking care of yourself is not an act of selfishness; rather, it is required for your own personal health and happiness. In order to revitalize your body and mind, you need get some exercise, consume nutritious food, spend some time outside, spend time with people who care about you, and enjoy their company.

Take care of your tension. The act of being shamed over one's appearance can be quite stressful. Building your resilience and keeping you from feeling overpowered by life's challenges can be accomplished with the help of relaxation strategies like exercise, meditation, and deep breathing exercises, to name just a few.

Accept the power that your body possesses. Every day, our bodies provide us the service of keeping us healthy and functioning at their best possible levels. Instead of being self-conscious about how you look, try to find reasons to be grateful for the "holy vessel" that you occupy. Take a moment to appreciate the remarkable capabilities that come naturally to you, such as the ability to breathe, the circulation of blood to the heart, and your senses. Your thoughts about your weight and your desire to be ideal are not related to the importance of making an effort to maintain a healthy body, which is the single most essential thing you can do.

Replace any negative self-talk with positive affirmations

Although you have no control over what other people say about you, you do have the ability to direct your attention to the positive aspects of who you are as an individual rather than fixating on any perceived shortcomings. The ability to recognize and accept one's own shortcomings is ultimately what will liberate one from the habit of passing unjust judgments on oneself or others.

Altering your internal monologue to include more positive thoughts and affirmations can be an effective strategy for elevating your mood and improving how you feel about your body and yourself.

Turn your attention to the qualities that you appreciate most about yourself. For instance, if you have gorgeous hair or eyes, this is equally as essential as the features that you don't like about yourself or that other people try to make fun of. When you next glance at yourself in the mirror, bring your attention to these admirable qualities.

Instead of constantly subjecting yourself to criticism, try accepting yourself without judgment. You may tell yourself anything along the lines of "I embrace my body just the way it is" or "My body is strong and healthy."

Feel proud of the unique person you are. Your worth as a human being is significantly more valuable than the sum of your bodily parts. The first step toward developing an acceptance of one's physical appearance is to reflect on the beneficial contributions that one makes to the world.

To begin, assume a neutral body position. You should strive toward attaining body neutrality if you are not yet ready to embrace the body positive movement. That you are accepting and respectful of your body even if you do not have to love or loathe it in order to reach this point. When you adopt body neutrality, you put the emphasis not on what your body looks like but on what it is capable of doing, rather than on how it looks. For instance, you could tell yourself, "Because of my legs, I am capable of walking and running for large distances."

Don't make fun of the bodies of others. According to a body of research, if you encourage body positivity to others, you will also experience an increase in your own sense of body positivity. Put yourself in an environment with people who are polite and respectful of the people around them. Stay away from bullies who make fun of other people's bodies and focus on the shortcomings of others.

Establish boundaries with the people in your social circle and make it abundantly apparent that you will not put up with comments about your physical appearance or weight. You can also set an example for others by defending those who are the subject of negative comments about their appearance.

Manage the amount of time you spend on social media

Spending an excessive amount of time on social media can increase your anxiety, loneliness, and dissatisfaction with your body. It can also reinforce unrealistic expectations that you have of yourself and put you at risk for cyberbullying and body shaming.

If you limit the amount of time you spend on social media, you will have more time to engage in other things that will improve your mood and allow you to more fully utilize your creative potential. Try:

In-person interactions with other people. If you want to increase the quality of your social connections, cutting back on your use of social media or completely stepping away from it can provide you the opportunity to engage with people in person. Face-to-face interaction is the antidote to stress that mother nature provides, and it can be significantly more satisfying than texting or messaging.

Activities such as walking, running, swimming, dancing, and other recreational sports are examples of physical activities. Being physically active is not only beneficial to your health and well-being as a whole, but it can also make you feel more confident, boost your self-esteem, and give you a sense of success.

Mindfulness can be practiced through activities such as yoga, meditation, deep breathing, or journaling.

Acquaint yourself with the food.

It is simple to form a perspective toward eating that is unhealthy when you are made to feel guilty or embarrassed about your weight. If you practice mindful eating, it will be easier for you to keep in mind that food is not the enemy and that you can find satisfaction in eating regardless of your weight.

To cultivate a positive relationship with food and to eat in a more thoughtful manner.

To get the most out of this pleasurable activity, put away all potential sources of distraction while you eat, such as your phone, the television, and any other activities that need you to perform multiple tasks at once.
You will be better able to taste each meal, eat more leisurely, and attend to the requirements of your body if you focus your attention on the here and now and embrace your thoughts and sensations. Making friends with food can also be accomplished by preparing wholesome meals in advance, as well as by preparing and testing out new dishes.

Reach out to a reliable friend or family member for advice and assistance.

There is no need for you to have to deal with this situation on your alone, despite the fact that you might be embarrassed to discuss the body shaming you've been subjected to with another person. Make an effort to connect with other people to receive advice and assistance, and be sure to fill them in on what you've been going through.

It is essential to locate a person in whom you have confidence and with whom you can open up about your emotions. You can find it easier to deal with the anguish and humiliation of being shamed about your body if you have a protected channel through which you can express your feelings.

Do not be reluctant to make an appointment with a certified mental health counselor or therapist if you feel as though you could benefit from additional assistance during the process of rehabilitation. They are able to provide objective guidance that will help you feel more in control of your life and heal from the impacts of body shaming.

Chapter 5

How to comfort a loved one who struggles with negative body images

Your compassion and understanding can be quite helpful to a friend or loved one who is experiencing body shame at the hands of others.

Make sure they understand that you are worried about them and how much you care about them. You may say something along the lines of "I feel sad when you speak adversely about your appearance" or "I am scared that you are often talking about your weight."

Maintain your composure and pay attention to their issues. Instead of assuming you already know what your loved one requires, ask them how you may help them out in the greatest way possible. It's possible that all they need is someone to lean on when they're feeling down, someone who will listen to their concerns without passing judgment.

You should make an effort to move the spotlight away from the physique of your loved one and onto something else about them that you enjoy. You may, for instance, bring up their fantastic sense of humor, how intelligent they are, their spirit of adventure, or highlight a particular talent that they possess.

Should your child have been subjected to body shaming,
Finding out that your child or teenager has been subjected to body shame can be an immensely painful experience. You can take action to deal with the issue, or perhaps help prevent it from occurring in the first place, just like you would with any other form of bullying or cyberbullying conduct.

Instruct your kid on the harmful effects of body shaming. You should explain to your child the importance of valuing and respecting both themselves and other people, as well as the fact that people can sometimes be unkind to one another. Remind them that criticizing someone's body in any way is completely inappropriate.

If the issue is taking place at your child's school, you should discuss it with the teachers and administration there.

In the event that your child's present friends engage in body shaming, you should encourage your youngster to look for new friends. Your child can significantly broaden their social circle by participating in extracurricular activities such as sports teams, youth clubs, and after-school programs.

Be a good role model. When you catch yourself saying something bad about your own appearance or physique, remind yourself to speak positively about your own body and body image. If you want to set a good example for others, try to use language that is either body-positive or body-neutral.

Limit the amount of time your child spends using various social media platforms. Keep an eye on the content that your youngster is reading and posting on their various social media channels. The more you are aware of your child's life online, the sooner you will be able to detect and address any difficulties related to body shaming that they may be experiencing.

Give your youngster reassurance. Give your child the assurance that you love them without condition, praising them for their inner as well as their outer attractiveness. Refrain from making jokes about a child's or adolescent's appearance while making fun of them or criticizing them in any way.

You should encourage your child to live a healthy lifestyle that nourishes their body, but you should avoid talking to them about topics such as their appearance, weight, and dieting. Instead, you should concentrate on the capabilities of your child's physical body. Involve them in activities that require them to use their bodies, such as running, jumping, drawing, playing an instrument, or solving puzzles.

Encourage your child to participate in physical activity and artistic pursuits so that they can build their self-esteem and resiliency. Getting them engaged in activities such as team sports, volunteer organizations, or other group activities can help them enhance their social skills and boost their self-confidence. Your child's mood can be improved by physical activity, which can also assist to alleviate worry and tension.

It is not always easy to avoid humiliating one's body, even if one makes every effort to surround themselves with positive people, messages, and positive internal dialogue. But, just as with anything else that drags us down, being aware of all the numbers and facts surrounding body shaming is a significant step toward overcoming it. There isn't nearly as much body shaming on magazine covers and in commercials, and people are more comfortable calling it out when they see it. The external forces that surround us appear to be improving. When it comes to prioritising self-care over attempting to be as slim (or whatever the current "It" body type it is), celebrities and media sources seem to be all about sending out the good vibes when it comes to having confidence in one's own body and promoting positive body image. And now days, we know it's a real movement because businesses are starting to get on board with it, and brands will only participate in a trend if they believe it will result in more profits for them.

Chapter 6

The truth about the practice of body shaming

It is not always easy to avoid humiliating one's body, even if one makes every effort to surround themselves with positive people, messages, and positive internal dialogue. But, just as with anything else that drags us down, being aware of all the numbers and facts surrounding body shaming is a significant step toward overcoming it. There isn't nearly as much body shaming on magazine covers and in commercials, and people are more comfortable calling it out when they see it. The external forces that surround us appear to be improving. When it comes to prioritising self-care over attempting to be as slim (or whatever the current "It" body type it is), celebrities and media sources seem to be all about sending out the good vibes when it comes to having confidence in one's own body and promoting positive body image. And now days, we know it's a real movement because businesses are starting to get on board with it, and brands will only participate in a trend if they believe it will result in more profits for them.

Popular clothing lines are adding more sizes to their racks and in their advertising so that we are not constantly confronted with images of people with the same body type. This is happening despite the fact that there is still a long way to go before all sizes can be considered fully inclusive. It is comforting to be reminded that there is nothing wrong with our "bikini bodies," that we do not need to cover up our flaws with concealer every morning, and that we are free to be as preoccupied with or as ambivalent as we want to be with our waistlines and haircuts.

Still, the body positivity movement can be problematic in its own right, particularly if you have been trying to overcome a lifetime of being bullied about your body, are recovering from an eating disorder, or simply can't help but not "love" the way you look in jeans. In these situations, it can be difficult to see the positive aspects of your body. According to the findings of a recent survey conducted by FitRated, the practice of body shaming is all too common, and it can originate from some unexpected quarters. The following is a portion of what they discovered:

Body shaming is something that happens to both men and women.
According to the survey, 93 percent of women and 83 percent of men reported having experienced body shame, which is a lot closer than we would have anticipated given the results of the survey. Although women also reported being ridiculed for their butts and lack of muscular tone, both men and

women said that their tummies and legs were the body regions they most frequently felt guilt about. Because of body shaming in the media, men reported feeling the need to have "chiseled" abs. This finding is interesting considering that some of the most famous and popular men in pop culture these days are adored for their "dad bods," even if they're not dads sometimes, while women who have actually given birth to children are harassed into "bouncing back" after a baby.

However, the effects of being shamed about one's physique might linger far longer for women. Although both women and men report experiencing body shame, the signals that women get about their bodies tend to affect them for a far longer period of time than those that males receive about their bodies. In point of fact, research conducted in 2016 discovered that as women and men become older, women report higher degrees of body shaming, whilst males start to report feeling more confident as they get older. The researchers came to the conclusion that this was due to the fact that in our society, it is more acceptable to comment on a woman's physique regardless of her age, whether she is 14 years old or 84 years old, whereas males are considered to be "just great" throughout their life.

Empathy is not something that can be gained via experience.

You would assume that the more we've been harassed and embarrassed about our bodies, the more inclined we are to speak up for someone else who is being shamed, but that's not necessarily the case. Sadly, such was not the case with the people who participated in this study. About one-third of those who had previously experienced being victimized by body shaming claimed to engaging in the practice themselves. Be polite, everyone!

The whole thing is your mother's fault.
It may come as a rude awakening to some, but it turns out that the media and popular culture are just two of the many institutions that are complicit in the practice of body shaming. The vast majority of people, including a staggering 62% of women and 30% of men, have claimed that their mothers had insulted their bodies in some way.

Even dads aren't much of a sweet treat. A bit more than forty percent of women and about twenty-six percent of males have claimed that their father has made them feel bad about their bodies in some way. As many of us probably are aware, grandmothers are also major perpetrators of body shaming. There were 35 percent of women and 17 percent of males who stated that their grandmother had told them a variety of unflattering things about themselves, including that they were too big, too little, too short, or too tall, amongst other things. The grandfathers of the respondents were excluded from the poll for reasons that are not clear.

And a variety of other unhealthy partnerships. In addition to their mothers, survey respondents reported being shamed by their significant others. However, this time around, the gender breakdown was not even close to being equal. Approximately half of women and one-quarter of males have claimed that their significant other has embarrassed them over their physique in some way. Some of the most significant reasons of body shame can also be found among close friends, sisters, and even brothers.

Thin-shaming is just as harmful as fat shaming in today's society.
Our society places a higher value on people who have smaller bodies since it is simpler for them to participate in public life, find nice clothes that fit, and even visit the doctor if they are thin. However, if you comment on someone's body in any way, including saying things like "you're so slender" or "like a stick," you could be engaging in the practice of body shaming. It is not up to the person making the comment to decide whether or not it is humiliating; that all depends on how the person who is listening to it feels, and you never know how your comment will land. People frequently say that their significant others have informed them that they are "too slim." This occurs with women just as frequently as it does with men. Both overcoming the practice of body shaming and achieving a positive outlook on one's own body can be

challenging. It's possible that it would be best if we all just quit talking about each other's bodies from the beginning.

Chapter 7

How to Love Your Body

It's possible that you fight an uphill struggle with food and your appearance every single day. Or maybe you just have the rare terrible day where you don't like what you see reflected back at you in the mirror.

In either case, engaging in combat with your own body is not a healthy state to be in. We've managed to become a culture that's fixated on the size and shape of our bodies, and it's gotten out of hand. Women suffer from this the most.

The journey toward loving and accepting your body completely might be a long one to travel. Believe me when I say that there is no easy way out of this predicament. However, there are several simple yet effective actions that you may perform on a daily basis to improve your connection to your physical self.

Learn to appreciate your physical self by following these steps (even when you sometimes hate it)

Admit that you do not currently have the kind of positive

relationship with your body that you would like (yet)

It's quite normal for you to be having a hard time loving your body right now. There are a good number of us.

You are aware of why...

Because we are currently living in a society that instills in us a deep-seated hatred for our physical selves. And if you make it through childhood uninjured, you can count yourself as one of the few rather than the many.

But the most essential thing is that you are conscious of the relationship that you currently have with your body and that you are accepting the fact that you want to make some adjustments. Because doing so is the initial step toward making a change.

Therefore, you must learn to accept the unfavorable relationship you have with your body. Also, admit that you wish to develop a constructive and wholesome one for yourself. Repeat this to yourself, and make sure you mean it.

Consider the reasons you want to present a different image.

This question is completely ignored by the vast majority of people since it never even occurs to them to consider it. Therefore, there is no better time than right now to contemplate the reasons behind your desire to present a new appearance.

What is the motivation behind your desire for your body to have a different shape or size?

Your motives are almost always deeply entrenched in the love and acceptance that you receive from other people. You have the misconception that if you had a body that is deemed more "beautiful" (whatever that term may imply), then other people will like you, respect you, or appreciate you more.

However, this is the most widespread misconception about the human body. Happiness cannot be achieved by altering one's appearance alone. It's possible that it could play a role in making you feel better about yourself, but by no means is it the only solution to the problem.

You need only take a glance at persons who have undergone cosmetic surgery or models who are naturally skinny to see that addiction and eating disorders are still a problem in today's society.

You have to let go of the assumption that attaining your ideal physique will solve all of your issues before you can begin to truly learn to accept the body you're in. Because if you don't confront the reasons why you don't feel good about yourself today, you will continue to carry those feelings with you until you do confront them and find a way to manage with them.

The only place to find genuine love and lasting pleasure is within yourself, as trite as it may sound.

Stop criticizing the appearance of the bodies of other people.

Do you spend your day critiquing the appearance of other individuals when you are out and about or while you are browsing through your phone?

When we behave in this manner, we give credence to the notion that our worth and value as human beings are directly correlated to the state of our bodies. However, they do not.

In addition to this, you continue to keep yourself in a state that is low-vibration and negative. This will have an influence on both your mood and your mental health, which you will then carry over into the rest of the day's activities and carry with you wherever you go.

I know that on some level, you are aware that you are deserving of being loved and accepted for who you are at this very now. That should be given to everyone. Therefore, let go of your judgment, because it isn't doing you or anyone else any good.

Tune in to your physical being and spend more time getting to know it.

Your body is similar to a long-time companion. You have known her since she was born, and it is essential that you spend sufficient quality time with her while being totally present with her; otherwise, your relationship will suffer from a deterioration in its strength and quality.

And there are a plethora of ways to do it, so you may truly inhabit your body and learn more about her.

Meditation is a wonderful technique to train yourself to be present and aware, as well as to help you feel more grounded. My practice of meditation often consists of going through the motions of scanning my body rather than focusing on my breathing. I'm going to close my eyes and start with my feet, and then slowly make my way up through the rest of my body. I'll devote some time to concentrating on each component, paying attention to any sensations or emotions that come up as a result. I'm not passing judgment on them; all I'm doing is raising awareness about them.

Tuning in to the rhythm of your menstrual cycle is yet another fantastic method to get to know your body on a deeper, more personal level. Start keeping a record of it, along with the changes in how you feel in your body at various times of your cycle. In addition, if you have period bleeding, you should think about trying a menstrual cup. You will become better acquainted with your blood, your vagina, and your cervix as a result of doing this.

Instead of focusing on your weight, you should shift your attention to things like love and compassion.

We've evolved into a society that's fixated on numbers on the scale. We demonize our bodies while simultaneously elevating them to a higher status than anything else in our lives. And we do this to ourselves by restricting our intake of food.

We eat to forget, to celebrate, to numb ourselves, to celebrate, to forget, to energize ourselves, and to boost ourselves up when we're feeling down on ourselves.

And as a result, we find ourselves mired in destructive patterns that we are either oblivious to or unwilling to break away from. Because we are so cut off from our bodies, we are unable to hear them when they try to communicate with us and tell us what they require and want. And even if we do, we still don't put our faith in them.

But until we stop believing that we are deserving of being punished, we won't be able to quit punishing ourselves. And in order to achieve that, you need to quit obsessing over the food you consume, the number that appears on the scale, and the number that is sewn into the waistband of your trousers.

What would happen if you made a shift and started focused all that energy on loving and compassionately directing it towards yourself instead of other people?

This is the essential step toward breaking the vicious cycle and gaining control over your weight once and for all. And when you do that, you will automatically start making decisions that are better for your health and more supportive of you.

Remove from your social media accounts everyone who makes you feel like you aren't good enough the way you are

I'm referring to all the "fitspo" and "thinspo" All of those attractive celebs you follow who always appear to have their make-up artists, personal trainers, and chefs at their beck and call. Anyone and everyone who posts images or stuff online that leaves you feeling inadequate or inadequately represented in some way.

The only way I could figure this out was by trial and error. When I originally started my company, I would frequently check Instagram and spend a good deal of time there. In addition to this, I was following a large number of women who were successful company owners and ran their own companies. But as time went on, I realized that being shown their highlight reel was making me feel terrible about who I was and what I was accomplishing, and it was all because of them.

Because there was always someone else who was more qualified. There was always someone who had greater success than I did. It caused me to forget about all of the wonderful things that I was doing and brought to my mind all of the things that I was not doing.

How heartbreaking is that!

And the same is true when considering one's weight and overall physical image. Your self-confidence and perception of your body will suffer if you are constantly bombarded with photos of people who have unrealistic body types or who have been extensively manipulated.

The truly mind-boggling part is that you are totally in charge of deciding which thoughts and pictures to let into your mind. You could stop following those accounts, delete the applications, reduce the amount of time you spend on your phone, and stop watching those television shows.

As a result, I want to encourage you to make decisions that are better for your health, more powerful, and more elevating.

Stop obsessing over your calorie intake and giving in to fad diets.

Do you believe that companies such as Slimming World and Weight Watchers would be experiencing the same level of growth in membership if calorie counting were effective?

Of course not. Because the information that they are teaching is ineffective, businesses like that continue to thrive.

They don't address the fundamental issue of why you have a poor connection with food in the first place, which is the basis of the problem. And they do not place an emphasis on or make efforts to encourage a healthy one. They push you to move from one extreme to the other, all the while maintaining the perspective that particular items are either excellent or harmful.

There is no such thing as good or evil. Consuming a diet that is both varied and well-balanced, as well as having an awareness of the nutritional significance of the foods one puts into their bodies, are essential to maintaining good health.

If you're wanting to improve the quality of your diet, the most effective strategy is to concentrate on consuming as many uncooked and unprocessed foods as you possibly can. fruits, vegetables, unprocessed grains and carbs, lean and unprocessed protein sources, nuts and seeds, and a variety of nut and seed butters. However, you shouldn't tell yourself that you can't occasionally indulge in items like pizza and ice cream when you have a want for them.

The practice of counting calories perpetuates the misconception that food is an adversary that must be monitored at all times, despite the fact that this is not the case. In the same way that your body is a magnificent gift from Mother Nature, so too is food.

Get your body moving in ways that are enjoyable to you.

I believe that the primary reason why so many of us choose not to exercise is because we have the misconception that it cannot be enjoyable. We have deceived ourselves into thinking that it needs to be difficult, unpleasant, and a chore; nevertheless, none of those things are true.

In point of fact, you ought to be able to enjoy yourself while doing it, and if you are unable to do so, then perhaps your strategy is flawed.

Moving your body in a way that makes you feel good will look and feel different for everyone because every body is unique. Because each of us has a little distinct neurological make-up. Don't bother going to the gym if you're the kind of person who, like me, finds the idea of working out at a gym repulsive.

You may begin doing yoga in your own house, or you could start going swimming. You might decide to begin running outside or take up belly dance and enroll in a class.

If you aren't sure what it is that you enjoy doing just yet, today is the perfect day to start trying out a variety of things. Continue on your journey until you find something that piques your interest, and once you do, engage in more of it.

Dedicate each day to performing at least one act of self-care.

When I say "self-care," I don't necessarily mean that it always involves activities such as giving yourself a facial, getting a massage, or drawing a bath for yourself.

There are times when practicing self-care means setting your alarm thirty minutes earlier so that you can make and savor a scrumptious, nutritious breakfast just for yourself. When your mind is telling you to give up, it is important to push yourself to stay in the plank position on your yoga mat for just two more breaths. This can be challenging at times. And there will be moments when you have to forego drinks with your pals in order to put in more time on the book you're writing.

You have to understand that practicing self-care isn't only about engaging in activities that provide immediate pleasure and nourishment. Doing things for yourself that you might not want to do but that you know your future self would be grateful for is another component of self-care.

If you are aware that you have difficulty loving your body, you should direct your attention toward your body when doing acts of self-care. And make it a daily priority to show your body some love by treating it to at least one act of self-care.

Remember to express gratitude for all that your body does for you on a daily basis.

We throw away a significant amount of time by ruminating on the aspects of our physical selves that we dislike.
What would happen if we changed our mentality and concentrated on the things that we really enjoy doing? Everything that happens on a daily basis within our bodies on our behalf. We need to be thankful for everything we have.

Not only will this put you in a more upbeat attitude, but it will also assist you in developing a new perspective regarding your physical appearance.

Therefore, give some thought to the things for which you are grateful.

The method in which your legs enable you to go from one location to another, and the way in which your eyes enable you to take in the breathtaking natural scenery that is all around you. The manner in which your arms enable you to cuddle a newborn infant to your chest when they are first born. And the method in which your lips are able to tenderly kiss the individuals who you care about.

Think about all of the power, beauty, and grace that is constantly flowing through your body. This happens every day. And remember to be grateful. Be appreciative.

Adorn your physical form with affection.

You should get rid of everything in your closet that is too big or too small for you, as well as anything that you've been wearing to hide your physique. Also, avoid purchasing clothing in sizes that you wish you could eventually fit into. This will just serve to perpetuate the notion that the current state of your body is not normal or acceptable.

Instead, you should treat your body as if it were a masterpiece and wear it in accordance with that mentality. Invest in some brand-new, well-fitting garments that not only look great on you but also make you and your body feel amazing if you are able to do so within your financial means. Whatever prints, colors, and accessories you find most eye-catching will look great on you.

Put an end to the notion that you won't be able to wear the way you want to until you reach a different size. Today, adorn your body with the love you feel inside. Because this is how you can learn to appreciate your body, even when you despise what it looks like.

In front of a mirror, say positive affirmations to yourself over and over again.

The things that we believe and the stories that we tell ourselves eventually become our truth and the reality that we produce for ourselves. Therefore, if you tell yourself that you are overweight, ugly, or useless, you will come to believe those things about yourself. In a similar vein, if you constantly remind yourself that you are a fucking badass Queen, you will eventually come to believe that you are.

Louise Hay was the first person from whom I learnt about the strong effects of mirror practice. You only need a mirror that reflects your entire body. If you can, place it so that it is slightly leaning against a wall, as this is the position that produces the most flattering angle.

Put yourself in front of your mirror naked first thing in the morning. Take a swig from your body, and try to come up with some complimentary things to say about it. You might want to concentrate on something that you actually enjoy, or you might want to concentrate on those aspects of it that are more challenging for you to appreciate.

Conceive of a reassuring affirmation for oneself, and speak it aloud to yourself on a regular basis.

In the same vein, if you're having trouble feeling the love, you shouldn't try to push it on yourself and you shouldn't be hard on yourself. It's okay if love feels out of reach right now; there's no rush to find it. You might be able to locate one or two things that appeal to you, though. Your eyes, your hair, or your fingers, whichever you like.

Surround yourself with people who will encourage you.

If you spend the majority of your time with individuals who do not love their bodies and who are always criticizing or judging themselves or others, then you will absorb the negative energy that they exude as if it were your own.

More than we realize, the individuals we spend the most time with have a significant impact on who we become. Because of this, it is essential that you surround yourself with optimistic and encouraging people. People who love and accept themselves exactly as they are, as well as people who love and accept you precisely as you are.

Whether it be family, friends, neighbors, or even coworkers, there is always someone to talk to. Take into consideration the people with whom you are spending time. It is important to not let fear prevent you from ending relationships that are no longer beneficial to the person you are developing into.

Do not be afraid to seek assistance when you need it.

It might be challenging to figure out how to appreciate your body when you despise it when you are attempting to do so on your own. Even if the logical part of you is aware of the many reasons why you should love your body, it may take more than just that for you to arrive to that place.

Investing in the services of a coach or therapist could be a life-changing decision for you at this point. There are professionals out there that have received specialized training in areas such as health, food, and nutrition; they provide both scientific and natural techniques, giving you options based on your personal preferences.

They will be able to guide and assist you on your path in a way that our friends and family members typically are not able to do.

Keep in mind that asking for assistance does not indicate that there is something wrong with you or that you have failed in any way. It takes a lot of guts and self-awareness to accept that you can't handle this on your own and to go ahead and seek for assistance. That should in no way bring you any sense of shame.

Always keep in mind that you have the ability to pick love over hate at any time.

At any given moment, you have the ability to choose to direct love rather than hate toward your body.

It's possible to rephrase "I loathe my body" as "I am working on creating a love relationship with my body."

It's possible that the phrase "My body is too fat" will eventually be replaced by "My body is exactly how it needs to be right now, and I am evolving."

It's possible to reframe "I can't eat that" as "I choose foods that nourish my body and fill me with energy to get me through the day."

You may say "I am on a journey to learn to appreciate and accept my beauty, both inside and out" instead of "I don't feel attractive."

Right now, you are the one in control. The situation has always been under your control. So, kindly return it right away.

Conclusion

Having self love for your body is the best thing you could ever do, you are beautiful, yes i'm talking to you. You are very beautiful, don't let what people say define you instead be in charge of yourself. Don't let anyone tell you that you are ugly or make you feel less than yourself. Be proud to be you, live your life because nobody is perfect.

www.ingramcontent.com/pod-product-compliance
Lightning Source LLC
LaVergne TN
LVHW030123160826
845673LV00019B/3005

* 9 7 9 8 3 7 0 9 8 7 1 5 1 *